SWING TRADI. _

A Beginner's Step by Step Guide to Make Money on the Stock Market With Trend Following Strategies

Descrierea CIP a Bibliotecii Naţionale a României
CARTER, MATTHEW G.

Swing Trading. Beginner's Step by Step Guide to Make
Money on the Stock Market With Trend Following Strategies. /
by Matthew G. Carter. - Bucureşti : My Ebook, 2018
  ISBN 978-606-983-593-7

336

SWING TRADING

A BEGINNER'S STEP BY STEP GUIDE TO MAKE MONEY ON THE STOCK MARKET WITH TREND FOLLOWING STRATEGIES

My Ebook Publishing House
Bucharest, 2018

CONTENTS

CONTENTS

INTRODUCTION

I want to thank you and congratulate you for downloading the book, Swing Trading: A Beginner's Step by Step Guide to Make Money on the Stock Market With Trend Following Strategies

This book contains proven steps and strategies on how to effectively to make money by Swing Trading successfully. This book is like a guide, it is a great dynamic list, that talks about timely signals, types of traders, the types of market involved, the trading signals. It's the result of study and research of the market and the keen observation into what works best to capture quick and profitable moves.

Thanks again for downloading this book, I hope you enjoy it!

Chapter 1

AN INTRODUCTION TO SWING TRADING

It is very important that to make money in the stock market; it is necessary to have a well-organized and disciplined methodology to trading. I also believe that it is also important as a vital rule to always keep things simple. So while our main goal is to keep things simple, the trading rules to making profits in the market though it may seem initially – a bit complex however, once you learn the rules of trading coupled with your being disciplined, you will make money in the stock market therein. Welcome to **Swing Trading**.

Before we delve more into the lands of swing trading, let us evaluate all of the other predominant types of styles of trading:

Scalping - The buyers in this type of trading aren't promoting their shares at all. As an alternative, they are purely in it for the small benefit. A scalper will make loads of trades a day, however handy, they make a small gain whenever they can. This approach is effective due to what is referred to as the bid-ask unfold. There is a little distinction between the best price a trader is willing to pay and the lowest charge for which a seller is inclined to sell it. It is a form of like a middle man kind of strategy. It takes some finesse to be a scalper, however not like the price tag scalpers you find seeking to make a quick buck from it all, the stock marketplace scalpers can make a variety of cash. Scalping may be enormously efficient for investors who pick to utilize it as an essential method, or even the people who utilize it to supplement exclusive types of broking. Clinging to the strict depart method is the manner to making little blessings compound into expansive will increase. The fast degree of market presentation and the recurrence of little actions are key traits which can be the reasons why this system is mainstream among several varieties of traders

Momentum buying and selling - A stock is said to have momentum when the stock charge starts to transport in one path and is accompanied by means of a high amount of trading magnitude. This strategy calls for the dealer to jump on board soon after the momentum begins after which it trips the wave for a while. Careful although live too lengthy and momentum ought to swing within the contrary course, but leap too quickly, and you could miss out on ability earnings. A happy medium is to set a favored profit and stop there. Please do, consider the kids.

Technical buying and selling/ Trading - Technical traders are passionate about charts and graphs, looking strains on stock or index graphs for signs and symptoms of convergence or divergence that might suggest purchase or sell signals.

Fundamental trading - The crux of fundamental buying and selling is analysis. The analysis is its core. Basics are the constructing blocks of a business, and their stock rate may be related to its sports. The evaluation comes in while a dealer examines the predicted impact of changes like stock splits, acquisitions, and profits reports. While accurate news might be assumed to be met with an upward push in stock rate, you never pretty realize how the market will react to any information – hence, use caution. Fundamental trading is just like normal buying and selling, but taking location in an exceptionally brief time frame.

Swing trading allows you to make money when the market is strong, soft, high or low or whether it is just going sideways. And this is why it could be said to be very advantageous than various other approaches to investing. The goal is to make high profits and money and not to rest your hopes on the future of a stock, the future of a sector, or that of an economy.

Chapter 2

SWING TRADING, WHAT IS IT?

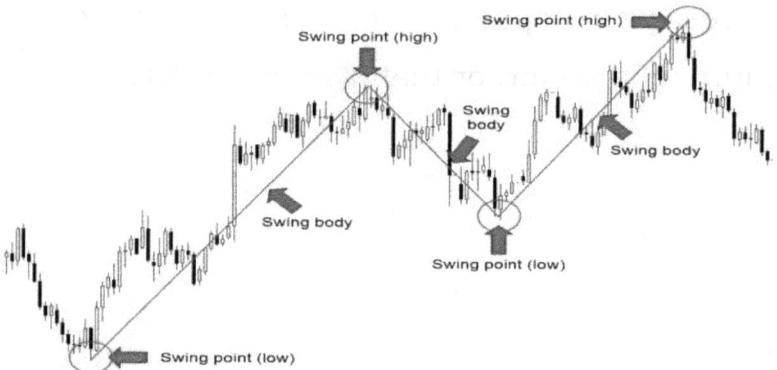

Without much talk so directly explain this term to the beginners in the stock market, just as the name implies, swing trading is the straight attempt to profit from the swings in the market. The highs and the lows. These swings comprise of two essential parts – the body and the swing point. In the image below, I will explain better.

I would say that swing trading is the kind of trading that in which positions are held for longer than a single day. This furthermore would mean that most fundamentalists (traders) are actually swing traders since changes in business principles generally require several days, a week or sometimes more than a week to cause sufficient price movements that render reasonable profits to different traders at that point in time.

It is therefore important to understand that the above description of swing trading is a simplification of the term. Totally in reality, the concept of swing trading sits rightly in the middle of the range flanked by day trading and trend trading. So a day trader will have to hold a stock anywhere from a few seconds to a few hours but never exceeds a day. Meanwhile, a trend trader examines the long-term fundamental trends of stock or index, and may also even hold the stock for a more extended period – for a few weeks or months. Now, swing traders (our primary focus) hold a particular stock for a period of time, generally a few days, 2 or 3 weeks, which is between those extremes, and they will trade the stock on the basis of its intra-week or intra-month fluctuations stuck between positivity and negativity.

So let us look at it like this, we all know what waves mean? Right? For those that don't understand what waves are, it could better be explained as alternates from positive to negative, then to positive and negative, and so on. You would be right to say fluctuations. Yes, you are right if you just said that. Waves are found everywhere. They are found in nature – you see waves on the beach, you see waves when you throw a stone into a lake – it moves in the current, now, that is wave. Sound is also transmitted in and by waves. Talking about stocks, in the stock market, when stock prices change, they follow a wave-like pattern. Waves are rare although they can be seen. They can be very slim, sometimes not seen but they are waves nevertheless, and we use these waves in Swing Trading. For swing trading styles, by differentiating, may have a couple of exchanges some days and nothing on others. Positions can be checked intermittently or taken care of with cautions when basic value focuses are come to instead of the requirement for consistent observing. This enables swing merchants to enhance their speculations and keep a leveled head while contributing.

Swing trading is truly one among the best and most efficient commercialism styles for a starting trader to get his or herself started in the stock market, and as a result, all you need to do is be straightforward. The rule of simplicity plays a big role here. And discipline that is. String trading nonetheless still offers significant profit potential for the intermediate to advanced traders. Swing traders, they receive sufficient feedback on their trades after a couple of days to keep them motivated in the market. Also, their long and short positions of holding for several days are of the duration that does not lead to distraction and by contrast, trend trading offers greater profit potential if a trader can catch a major market trend of weeks or months. This position, however, is mostly seen or caught by a few traders who are the traders with sufficient discipline to hold a position for that stretched period of time without getting distracted.

Alternatively, trading of dozens of stocks per day which is day trading may just prove to be quite a huge Herculean task far too great for some traders, thereby making swing trading the perfect medium between the extremities of the stock market.

THE STEPS IN SWING TRADING

AN INTRODUCTION TO TRENDS

Trading, we all want to start trading and making profits from stocks or our investments, but there are some things that you may need to know before starting to swing trade. As I always say, *MAY THE SWING BE WITH YOU.* So the things that you will need to get acquainted with is called **'trends'** and they are divided into two types. They are the uptrend and the down trend. In an uptrend, we usually notice it by a series of higher highs and higher lows (the bottom of each pull-back). Now to make your profits or increase your chances of making it, you buy on the **pull-backs**. According to Larry Swing, a famous swing trader, he defines an uptrend, saying that it is a series of successive rallies stating that with each rally going higher than the previous one and each pull-back stopping above the previous one. In other words, the person that can predict the pattern of this trend in swing trading is who makes a maximum profit or any at all. To better understand string trading if you haven't gotten the hang of it yet, what you should know is that swing buyers are not seeking to hit the home run with an unmarried alternate – they are no longer worried about perfect timing to buy a stock precisely at its bottom and promote exactly at its top (or vice versa). Preferably, in an ideal trading surrounding, they look ahead to the inventory to hit its baseline and confirm its course before they make their actions.

The story of swing tradings uptrend gets extra complicated while a more potent uptrend or downtrend is at play: the trader might also ironically cross long whilst the inventory jumps underneath its EMA and anticipate the stock to move returned up in an uptrend, or she or he can also fast a stock that has stabbed above the EMA and waited for it to drop if the longer trend is down. Better yet, technical brokers/traders' most objective is to recognize a solid uptrend and to benefit from it until the point when it inverts. Offering an advantage once it has neglected to make another pinnacle or trough is a standout among other approaches to keep away from the substantial misfortunes that can come about because of a turned around slant. Numerous technical merchants will likewise attract trendlines to recognize an uptrend and will utilize this instrument as a guide for when to offer as it can likewise be an early sign of a pattern inversion.

A DOWN TREND is noticing that after the price moves down, it also takes a rest, or pulls up. The price in the stock chart follows a movement depicting a zigzag pattern. The downtrend can be identified by a series of lower lows and lower highs ultimately, the peak of each pull-up. If you want to make a profit while swing trading, you should sell short during a pull up.

So not all technical traders use trend lines. I know it may seem too technical and somewhat difficult at the beginning of your trading, but once you look at it with patience and discipline, you will understand it all. If I have to be honest, I will have to say that I have no idea why anyone would ignore them – they are very important –

mostly as a swing trader – DISCIPLINE. So take note of these things.

THE STEPS TO FOLLOW WHEN YOU WANT TO TREAD THE RIGHT PATH OF STRING TRADING, you will need to do it in these steps below. I will try to be as simple as possible, so I will give them to you in bullet points. It is not rocket science as it can be followed. Once again, with patience and discipline (always have these in your mind).

The first thing to note is that you will need to restrict your selection to the category of stocks that willsatisfy certain criteria. Getting that in mind, let's start;

So pick stocks;

+ That have a least price of at $7

+ They should also have an average daily volume of at least 500,000 shares

✓Once all the above has been checked, follow the steps below.

STEP 1 – You will need to be able to spot a stock that has its way in an uptrend or downtrend,

STEP 2 – So now, for stocks in an uptrend, you will need to spot the particular stocks that are experiencing a pull-back and for a downtrend, look for stocks and spot the ones that are experiencing a pull-up.

STEP 3 – Once an appropriate candidate (stock that has passed the test of being in an uptrend or downtrend) is marked, you should place a limit order to buy (uptrend) or also sell short (downtrend) the stock based on the already explanation aforementioned.

STEP 4 – Once a stock has been successfully traded (a position opened), you will place a stop-loss order to limit downside risk and place a limit order so as to identify the price at which you will take profits. (Ideally, these two orders are placed together as an OCO (One Cancels Other, or One Cancels the other if you please) order; this is sometimes called an OCA (One Cancels All) order. In other words, mean that one order can cancel all.

STEP 5 – At the end of each day, adjust the stop loss prices.

Swing Trading Systems

Swing buying and selling isn't always for everybody. Not like conventional stock choosing. Swing investors commit a lot of their time to making income inside the brief period and for a lot of people, it is their job.

Expert scrutiny has lead swing investors towards a greater systematic method. Swing trading structures particularly take the shape of stock charts. Those charts help the professionals perceive what is occurring inside the marketplace in a statistically sizable way. Styles like help or resistance show that a stock isn't probably to hold, shifting past a positive most or minimal price. Those limitations aren't the same for all shares. However, they are determined by using elements like the inventory's historical performance and general market tendencies.

Predicting inventory expenses based on beyond traits isn't any simple undertaking. If it did, absolutely everyone could make a killing on the stock market. We know that is no longer the case however why? This is because it seems that human behavior can be extraordinary sometimes and while humans soar at the bandwagon shares, can move way up or down because of the masses behavior. And at the end of the day, investing in stocks is risky, and the prospect of losing your clothing keeps most of the people honest.

Chapter 3

PATTERN RECOGNITION CRITERIA

Pattern recognition is one of the maximum versatile talents you can research in relation to buying and selling of stocks in string trading of the stock market. Sure, the spending of time concentrating on the analysis of charts and its styles can often let you know whether a stock is a proper candidate for swing trading. However, it is very time consuming to study those charts in particular, if you search for candidate possibilities each day. Every other way to become aware of top stocks is to use softwares which could test all the listed stocks based totally on a chain of algebraic equations that represent the traits of an excellent chart pattern. You could use a **swingtracker** to perform this mission. That will be further explained in the forthcoming chapter titled *what tools are available?*

Knowing that there are various approaches of pattern popularity standards, let us, in brief, speak the measures which use the algebraic equations. Some of the measures, there are simple descriptive variables (examples are visible in the excessive prices seen within the previous day or the inside the common quantity over the past 20 days). Other measures are based on technical evaluation of shares.

Another measure is that of technical evaluation. It has many special indicators starting from the simplest of movement among the average up to complex oscillators. It is also now not just vital to have an in-depth knowledge of technical analysis to be a successful swing trader, but it is far helpful to have a rudimentary expertise of the way we approach swing trading sample popularity.

Technical Analysis Measures used to Recognize Swing Trading Patterns

Initially, I would say that we should typically restrict our picks to shares which can be at a minimum of $12 in fee, in other words, they must be having a mean of (20 days) each day volume of as a minimum 500,000 shares. Because marketplace makers can greater without difficulty manipulate the low price, low quantity stocks, we stay away from them.

For lengthy swings we are interested in identifying stocks that are in an uptrend. One of the signs we use is a Simple Shifting Common

(SMA). A transferring common is truly the common closing price for a particular range of days. It's known as a transferring common because on each new day, the contemporary day's fee is added to the average even as the oldest rate is dropped. We usually open awareness on three shifting averages, those based totally on 10 days, 20 days and 50 days. All shifting averages ease the price motion and make it simpler to perceive trends. It's also sizable to know in which today's rate is relative to the shifting averages and whether the shorter time frame transferring common is above or below, the longer time body moving average. Signs that a stock is in an uptrend are:

• Today's closing charge is above each the 10-day and 20-day shifting averages

• The 10-day shifting average is above the 20-day moving common

While searching out a long swing, we would like to discover stocks which are experiencing a quick decline (pullback). We can discover a 3-day pullback as follows.

• Nowadays' excessive charge is decrease than the day before today's excessive.

• Yesterday's high is lower than the high of the previous the day.

I also use a technical indicator evolved by Dr. Alexander elder known as the pressure index. This index combines the magnitude of the fee trade with the path of the trade and the trading volume. With a view to verify the relative pressure in the back of an uptrend and a pullback, we use a 3-day shifting common and a thirteen-day shifting common of the force index. The following conditions display that the bears were winning the short-time period struggle while bulls are dominating the longer frame:

- The 3-day moving common of the pressure index is less than zero, and
- The 13-day shifting average of the pressure index is more than 0

Every other technical indicator I like to use is the **Directional Movement Index** (DMI) that became advanced by means of J. Welles wilder Jr. Its miles used to decide whether or not an inventory is trending or no longer trending (that is, shifting sideways). In the **swingtracker** software, it offers the two additives of this indicator – the high quality directional index (+di) and the terrible directional index (-di) – along with a 20-day transferring common based on these measures (adx). An uptrend is confirmed if:

- adx is better than 30
- +di is better than –di

Chapter 4

THE MASTER PLAN. WHAT IS IT?

The Master Plan is described as a set of rules that determine when to go into the market to trade –buy and sell stocks. At the beginning of it all, it might seem like there is a little hint of complexities in the whole thing, you will however, realize – you will notice fast that – they were in actual fact, really quite easy –well after you recognize. The notable trouble about the keep near plan is that which you don't want to use judgment. The pointers are mechanical. Barriers to a fulfillment searching out and selling are the human feelings of worry and greed. Through using ways of following the draw close to plan, the one's feelings will not have an impact on your conduct, nor will they intervene collectively together on the facet of your success.

To maintain it smooth, we will first focus on the prolonged change. The suggestions for a quick alternate are the reflected photo of the recommendations for an extended change. An example of an extended swing possibility is examined beneath. The fee has declined (pulled lower lows yet again) and bullish on the inventory.

An important characteristic of the draw close to plan is setting an earning purpose and maintaining capital. The technique within reason conservative – the profits purpose is ready 7 per cent with a functionality loss capped at four per cent. The real profits are probably to be greater than 7 per cent on the equal time as a loss might be to be smaller than 4 per cent. The way here is the way it certainly works.

• As fast due to the fact the aim charge is reached (7 per cent above the access price), half of the shares are sold, locking in a 7 per cent profit. The possibility stocks stay invested to advantage from any similar boom in price.

• If the price movements in opposition to the alternate, the maximum loss tolerated is 4%. This preserves capital for future trades.

• Commonly, extra trades will produce a profit than a loss. The net surrender give up result is profit.

• The motion of the complete market may be very powerful at the same time as the market is shifting along element your trades, a very excessive percent of your trades may be worthwhile.

• Even as the whole marketplace is transferring in competition for your change, a better than expected percentage of your trades will lose. The prevent loss protects you from immoderate losses.

Chapter 5

THE RIGHT MARKET

Actions now and then have unintentional consequences, most times, no one knows how a string of events carry out to play irrespective of the planning. The meaning of this is that no one has means of actually knowing for certain what began or can begin a series of events, better put; string of events – due to the fact you can only usually leap one more hyperlink in that chain again. It is a perpetual fowl-egg state of affairs. These unintentional outcomes are commonly not what swing traders use to model their techniques.

For instance, when the occasions of Sept. 11 transpired, something peculiar happened to a product you wouldn't count on. Pajama sales skyrocketed after Sept. 11 because people have been much less inclined to head outside. This effect is higher referred to as cushioning.

The indicators that swing investors use to make trades often should do with statistical records. Swing buyers use charts to devise this information in a manner that they could expect positive tendencies. One of the most vital signs is volume. Volume refers to the wide variety of man or woman stocks being traded over a selected period. For swing buyers, that length is often a day. While quantity will increase, its miles a signal to traders that there is abruptly more excitement approximately a stock. However, the charge won't circulate right away, but the pleasure is not for not anything - eventually, the rate will both rise or fall sharply.

This approach is known as on-stability volume, or OBV for brief. It is an essential device for any swing trader to learn.

It must be stated that in either of the two marketplace extremes, the bear-market surroundings or raging bull marketplace, swing buying and selling proves to be as an alternative exceptional project than in a market that is between these extremes. In those extremes, even the maximum lively shares will no longer showcase the same up and down oscillations that they might while indexes are incredibly strong for some weeks or months. In a bear market or a raging bull marketplace, momentum will commonly bring shares for a long time period in one route most effective, thereby confirming that the satisfactory strategy is to alternate on the premise of the longer-term directional trend.

The swing trader, therefore, is greatly located when markets are going nowhere – when indexes upward thrust for more than one days and then decline for the following couple of days simplest to repeat the same well-known pattern over and over again. A couple of months would possibly pass with important stocks and indexes more or less the same as their authentic levels. However the swing trader has had many possibilities to trap the quick term actions up and down (sometimes inside a channel).

Of direction, the trouble with each swing buying and selling and long term fashion buying and selling is that fulfillment that is based totally on effectively figuring out what type of marketplace is presently being experienced. Trend buying and selling might be the suitable strategy for the raging bull market of the final half of the Nineties, while swing trading likely might have been best for 2000 and 2001.

Chapter 6

WHAT TOOLS ARE AVAILABLE?

In the preceding chapters, we have gone together step by step on what string trading is, how you can go about it, the types of traders, trading styles, the types of market and so on and so forth. All these are good because, for a beginner trader, you need to learn the basics and to be briefed on what string trading is in the stock market. That being said, without much time, we will also briefly cover the tools that are used to carry out safe and successful trading whether it is a sell short or not. The only goal is to make maximum profit. To do that, you will need to be acquainted with the prevalent tools available for this enterprise. I have searched through the World Wide Web and discovered some of the most satisfactory resources to use. This list is by no means a comprehensive list of the tools that can be used. There are others. So please feel free to search out for more. But before then, the following are the researched list of swing trading software for technical analysis of stocks.

Swing Tracker: Is a real time charting program that can be used to catch swings when they show themselves. The software works in such a way that it does scans. The software can be found at www.mrswing.com. It was designed to identify swing trading opportunities. Just as SwingTracker has many features, the scan feature, one of its many features, is used to identify stocks whose price action show patterns that present them as good candidates for swing trading.

The scan feature allows you to identify patterns based on price history, volume history, moving averages, technical indicators, candlestick criteria, and fundamental company characteristics. Scan criteria are saved in a scan library so they can be used over and over again. A scan scenario (also called a template) can be used to evaluate patterns in over 6000 stocks on the NYSE, the AMEX, and the NASDAQ. This evaluation happens in real time.

During the day, you can make use of the SwingTracker to monitor the price and volume behavior of individual stocks. You can easily monitor stocks on favorites.

Trade Miner: This software application tells you exactly which stocks have traditionally been winning trades all through the modern month. It additionally tells you exactly what day to shop for and what day to sell to make a profit.

Market Club: This service is right for charting, scanning, and buying and selling all in one. It additionally suggests more than one signs and lets you draw trend strains.

Finance software: Loose financial recommendation, private economic software, accounting software program, making an investment software, actual property software program and greater. Attempt your hand at all unique sorts of investing and get assist loose.

Technical analysis, it is a trading tool utilized to assess securities and endeavors to speculate their future development by dissecting measurements accumulated from exchanging action, for example, value development and volume. Not at all like basic investigators who endeavor to assess a security's inherent esteem, technical examiners concentrate on graphs of value development and different explanatory apparatuses to assess a security's quality or shortcoming and figure future value changes.

I hope with all these, you will swing in the right direction. I would love to hear your thoughts on the book.

CONCLUSION

Thank you again for buying this book!

I hope this book was able to help you to understand better what string trading means, the types of market trading, the different styles that can be implemented, and the types of tools available to the string trader and most especially, knowing the right indicators to buy, sell or hold.

The next step is to please go and give me a review. It will be very helpful for people who are still trying to decide on whether they should buy or not. Thank you.

Finally, if you enjoyed this book, then I would like to ask you for a favor, would please be kind enough to leave a review for this book? It'd be greatly appreciated! Please kindly put in a good word of the knowledge you just acquired.

Thank you and good luck! May the swing be with you!!!

P.S. Happy *(swing)* trading

Preview Of 'Momentum Stocks'

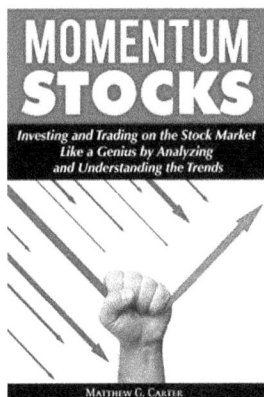

This book has actionable information on how to invest and trade on the stock market like a genius by analyzing and understanding the trends.

"The trend is your friend"

You've probably heard this saying before; of course it's one of the oldest sayings in the stock trading and investing world but what you might not know is that this saying is a shorter version of a longer sentence. The fuller version is actually *"The trend is your friend, until the end when it bends!"*

This full version affirms that there are two types of trend traders- those who follow the trend and make profits, and those who follow the trend, make profits and then lose it in the end.

Which of these traders do you want to be?

Trend trading is certainly a good thing- people like John. W. Henry earned millions of dollars from trend trading. From the proceeds of his investments, he bought the Boston Red Sox and the Liverpool Football Club and today, he is worth over $2.2billion.

The truth is that trend following is a very controversial topic; many financial advisors would advise you to stay off trend stocks, and that they don't work for stocks but people like John. W. Henry have proven them wrong.

People who tell you to stay off trend following simply have no idea about how to trade trend stocks; there are methods to these things ,and in this book, you're about to learn some of the secret strategies that successful trend traders use.